Composition and Perspective

T.W. WARD

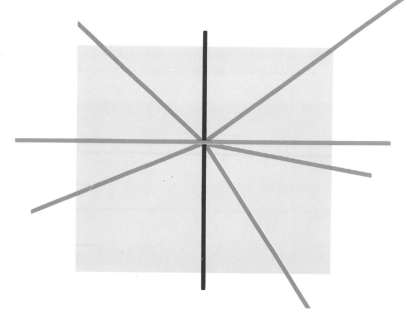

Series Editor
Ken Howard

First published in 1988 by
Bloomsbury Publishing Limited
This edition published 1991 by
Magna Books, Magna Road, Leicester, UK, LE18 4ZH
Reprinted 1992, 1993
Produced by the Promotional Reprint Company Limited
Copyright © Swallow Publishing Ltd. 1988

Note: Throughout this book, American terms are signalled in
parenthesis after their British equivalents the first time in
each section they occur. In frame and artwork measurement,
height always precedes width.

ISBN 1 85422 194 9

Printed and bound in Hong Kong

Contents

Foreword

'Of course, it is a gift.'
This is another of those common expressions which deter people from becoming involved in drawing and painting, although they would dearly love to.

No one believes that the ability to write is a gift given to a few people only. Most people take it for granted that they can write, albeit on a fairly basic level. Yet many people still believe that the ability to paint is something you have or you don't, that it is a gift that touches just a few. However, people have spent many pleasurable hours painting and much good painting has been produced without that divine gift.

To learn to write requires the discipline of learning grammar and practising the marks, and drawing and painting require the same disciplines. This book has been designed to introduce you to some of this basic grammar.

Art Class is a series of titles geared specifically to the requirements of the amateur painter. Some of the books are technique-based to help you to acquire first the basic, then the more advanced, techniques you need to enable you to work in a particular medium. Others are subject-based, outlining the theory and principles which you should understand in order to produce pleasing and technically adept works of art. All are full of sound practical advice, and suggest exercises and projects which you can do in order to gain a clear understanding of the subject. All the writers involved in the series, as well as being professional artists, have at some time in their careers been involved in teaching in art schools; indeed I have had the pleasure of teaching with several of them myself.

The most difficult element to grasp in drawing and painting is composition, or the arranging of the parts into a whole. In painting a landscape, for example, it is relatively easy to draw a building, or a tree or a fence, but fitting them together into a coherent landscape is the hard part, and it is here of course that the element of perspective clearly enters into the problem.

At one time, every art student had to learn the fundamentals of perspective. It was never an easy process so it could not just be touched on, it had to be learned thoroughly, and yet it was a discipline which every student came to understand. The fundamentals of composition were also taught, as was an understanding of the principles of the Golden Section or divine proportion. What we learned with time was that through

T. W. Ward 'Hauled Out for a Polish' 624 × 477mm (25 × 19in.).

practice these disciplines could eventually become intuitive. By understanding the Golden Section it becomes part of one's sensibility, by understanding perspective it is eventually part of one's way of seeing which one can use, discard, or bend according to one's understood needs.

Bill Ward's book is a very thorough explanation of the fundamentals of composition and perspective. It analyses thoroughly both disciplines and will give to anyone who is truly interested in a serious understanding of picture making a solid base on which to practise and build.

Bill Ward is an enthusiast and he has a real enthusiasm for picture making. Read his book, grasp the nettle and you will find his enthusiasm catching.

Ken Howard

5

Introduction

This vase from the fourth century BC is an example of the Greeks' use of perspective.

(Artist unknown) Japanese print 370 × 228mm (14½ × 9in.). None of the traditional Western methods of creating form by using tone or perspective has been used in this print. Emotion is expressed through the conflicting and powerful angles of the flat design.

Composition and perspective are powerful tools in artists' hands, once you have understood how to employ them. They are both concerned with the way that shapes and forms are ordered on the page and with creating works that make visual sense to the viewer and which have in-depth structure.

Composition is the organization of the shapes and forms into an expressive whole, whereas perspective produces the illusion of three dimensions on a two-dimensional surface. In most Western art the two work together, in a relationship that can perhaps be understood by an analogy with literature. In this, the role of perspective is like that of grammar, and composition like that of vocabulary. The compositional elements – line, shape, tone and colour – need to be ordered into coherent phrases and sentences, and this is the function of perspective – reproducing those elements in a form that can be 'read'. The roots of the two words also throw some light on their meaning. Composition derives from the Latin *compositus*, which means well-arranged, whereas perspective comes from a word concerned with looking – *perspicere*, to look through.

An artist, then, uses composition and perspective to present a coherent pictorial representation of elements of life and scenery from the world of our visual experience. Composition is present in any painting, from the moment you put two blobs of colour down next to each other, but perspective has only been conventional in painting from the late Middle Ages, and was to remain so until the early years of our own century. It is still a powerful tool in representational art. Simply put, perspective enables us to differentiate between forms of different sizes and at different distances from the viewer and to grasp immediately what those relationships are. Take a simple drawing by a child of two people against a background. The child will probably draw the two people in different sizes against some other objects, and it will not be possible to tell whether the smaller of the two is merely smaller than the other one, or is the same size, but is further away. Perspective enables you to establish such relationships in your work.

Although formal rules of perspective were not developed until the Renaissance, a simple form was known earlier. It was used by the Greeks in decorations on their pots and by the Romans in the mural paintings in their villas. But the Renaissance architects' use of space in their great buildings

challenged painters to find a means of equalling this concept of space on a two-dimensional surface, and this led to the great discoveries in perspective.

A study of perspective alone, however, does not make a work of art more (or less) beautiful. For centuries artists managed without it and more recently, since the experiments of the Cubists and the consequent development of abstraction, many artists have had no need for it. However, if you want to produce drawings and paintings that represent the visual world as you see it, a grasp of the principles of perspective will be invaluable.

The studies of composition and perspective are equally applicable, whether you are drawing or painting, but for this book the more direct approach will be studied through drawing. As in most disciplines knowledge and understanding give confidence, and in art this is as important as observation and sensitivity to form and colour. As you gain an improved understanding of these principles, you will find that your work will gain in confidence and that you will be better able to create a finished work from your sketches.

Valerie Thornton 'Cley Hall Farm' 400 × 572mm (15¾ × 22½in.). This sensitively balanced etching illustrates how depth is created without resorting to perspective in a composition in which the forms have been flattened, creating an almost abstract design. Depth is achieved by tone, and the scale of the textures. The carefully calculated lines on the left of the design are less intended to contribute to the feeling of depth than to give variation to the shapes created by the vertical and horizontal structure of the etching.

Many amateur artists and students fear that perspective is an abstruse subject, but in fact a grasp of the three-dimensional world is fundamental to our existence, and also to the mechanics of the eye and the way we perceive. It is a very straightforward process to gain a working understanding of the principles and to be able to use them to solve most visual problems concerning the size of shapes in distance. This book aims to teach the basic rules which will solve most problems, and at the same time to convey the principles of composition. It does this through giving a series of exercises, which are designed to be followed and put into practice. If they are read on the page without being tried out, they may sometimes appear to be complex and difficult, but if you actually do the drawings yourself, you should find that they are quite straightforward.

Another word of warning is to do them in sequence. They are designed to follow from one another, and if you skip or dip you may find that you are missing a vital piece of information that was given earlier.

Ultimately, however, your surest route to expressing the third dimension successfully in well-composed works is intense observation of your subject, careful study of angles and relative shapes and a feeling for space. Mastery of composition and perspective does not derive from learning a series of rules to which you have to adhere slavishly, but from the knowledge that gives the confidence to respond with spontaneity and excitement to the beauty of things you see around you.

'Hauled Out for a Polish'. This chalk study for a painting was done to establish the composition. The original view of the boats that I had was horizontal. From this study, however, I decided that a vertical shape was more appropriate for the purpose of the finished painting, which was to emphasize the unstable shape of boats out of the water.

Materials and equipment

A few simple tools will be needed to practise the exercises in this book: an A2 (594 × 420mm/23½ × 16½in.) or ½ imperial (541 × 417mm/21¾ × 16in.) drawing board; A2 (594 × 420mm/23½ × 16½in.) white cartridge (drawing) paper; flat-headed drawing pins or masking tape for securing the corners of your paper to the board; a T-square to fit your drawing board; a 45° and 30°/60° set square (triangle), preferably of thick plastic and no less than 200mm (8in.) along the longest side – thin plastic bends and is liable to slip under a ruler or T-square; a pair of compasses for taking off measurements; H or F (2½–3) grade pencils – softer grades smudge easily; a 300mm (12in.) ruler – again, plastic is preferable to wood.

To use your instruments correctly requires no special skills. Hold your T-square arm hard up against the left side of your board to draw a horizontal line at any height across the board.

Slide the set square along the T-square, or along a firmly held ruler, or hold it underneath a horizontal line to locate the centre of vision and vanishing points of either a 45° or 30°/60° projection. The larger you make a perspective drawing with instruments, the easier you will find it to be accurate.

A useful hint when you are drawing a line to get it just where you want it is to put the point of a sharp pencil on the exact place you wish to start the line, slide your ruler, T- or set square up to it until it touches, then draw along. This is a great deal easier than trying to put the ruler in exactly the right point first.

Always keep your instruments clean, otherwise your drawing soon becomes dirty.

To prevent a plastic ruler or set square sliding about independently, stick a narrow strip of masking tape along the back.

You won't need a vast array of tools and equipment to practise the perspective exercises in this book: the most useful items are illustrated here.

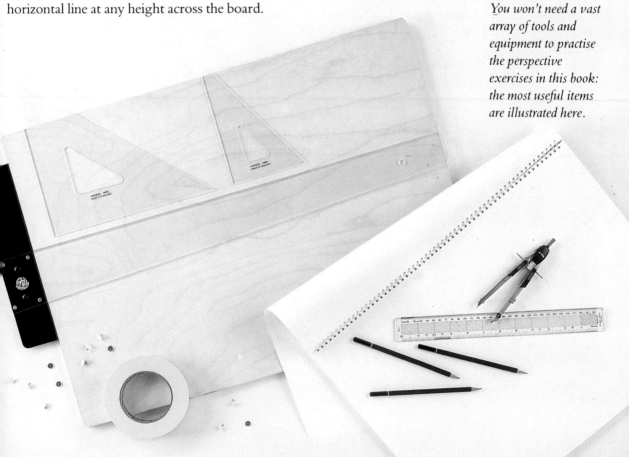

1 Composition

In his 'Notes on the Art of Painting' given to the Royal Academy in 1783 Sir Joshua Reynolds wrote:

'Composition, which is the principal part of the invention of a Painter, is by far the greatest difficulty he has to encounter. Every man that can paint at all, can execute individual parts; but to keep those parts in due subordination as relative to a whole, requires a comprehensive view of the art, that more strongly implies genius, than perhaps any other quality.'

In spite of Reynolds' rather pessimistic view, the principles of composition – arranging shapes within the picture area – once understood, can be mastered to good effect.

Sir Joshua Reynolds 'Self Portrait', painted 1753 or 1754.

The shape of the surface

For most artists the flat, two-dimensional surface is the stage on which they act out and convey all their emotional and intellectual ideas. Therefore, the size, shape and proportion of this surface have an important effect on a picture.

Artists' papers, boards and canvases are available in a very wide range of sizes and proportions and if you are making up your own canvases from stretchers there is an even greater choice of size. There is no objection either to cutting a board or piece of paper to the size and shape you would like it to be, so there is no need to feel inhibited by materials that come in stock sizes. You can work to any size and shape you feel comfortable with.

One of the most common shapes for easel paintings is the horizontal rectangle (diagram 1). Since its base is greater than its vertical sides, it produces a very stable shape. One feels it would be difficult to knock it over. The eye can roam

Diagram 1. The horizontal (or landscape) rectangle.

'Dangerous Reef' 485 × 700mm (19 × 27½in.). The powerful line of the horizon in this long composition is offset by the curves of the waves and the stern plates to exploit fully the overall shape.

Diagram 2. The vertical (or portrait) rectangle.

Cosimo Tura 'The Virgin and Child Enthroned' 2390 × 1016mm (94¼ × 40in.). This painting shows Tura's mastery of design and creative use of perspective. He exploits the vertical format to the full, by repeating the arch at the top of the painting with the niche in which the Madonna sits, and underlining the height of the throne by the supporting figures and pillars on each side, which are emphasized by the two figures beneath.

expansively from side to side and also back into the picture (this is termed 'recession'). This has been and still is a favourite shape of the English and Dutch landscape painters, among them John Constable, J. M. W. Turner, and Meyndert Hobbema; indeed it is known as 'landscape' shape in art circles. However, it does not invite the eye to travel up and down.

The same rectangle up-ended (diagram 2) presents a very different feeling. It is less stable and could be knocked over easily, the eye cannot move much from side to side and is inhibited from going deep into the shape. However, the eye can roam up and down. It can soar, and consequently this became the favourite shape of the great religious painters, like Botticelli, Crivelli, and Tura, whose subjects like the 'Assumption of the Virgin', or 'Christ in Majesty' or the 'Ascension' were perfectly conveyed by this format. It has also been the format of descents into Hell and a hilarious drawing of a Royal Academy soirée by Rowlandson of an avalanche of inebriated members and their ladies tumbling down the main staircase. It is not such an easy shape to fill as the landscape, but is ideal for portraits and has earned the name throughout the art world as 'portrait' shape.

The square (diagram 3) is the least evocative and most neutral shape, although it has great stability. It invites the viewer to look into its centre and the eye tends to roam in a spiral around that point. This tendency was exploited by the great

Venetian painters, Veronese and Tintoretto, the former in 'Unfaithfulness' from his 'Allegory of Love' series and the latter in 'The Origin of the Milky Way'. More recently, Pieter Mondrian used the square because of its neutral qualities and relied upon his sensitivity to shape and the space within it to overcome that inherent neutrality.

The diamond shape (diagram 4) has little equilibrium; it is just balanced and presents a challenge to the artist to create a balanced stable design within it. More complex variations of shape than even the diamond are being tried today, with artists assembling different shapes and sizes of canvases to produce very large paintings of dynamic and arresting designs.

The final shape we will look at is typical of a painting designed for an architectural setting (diagram 5). Its half-round, arched top cuts off the top corners of the rectangle, but artists frequently incorporate the surrounding architectural features outside the picture area as anchorages and fulcrums for the main directional lines when employing this shape.

Paolo Veronese 'Unfaithfulness' 1850 × 1850mm (74 × 74in.). In this brilliant example of the square format, vertical and horizontal lines through the centre of the picture intersect where the figure's hip joins her torso.

Diagram 3.
The square.

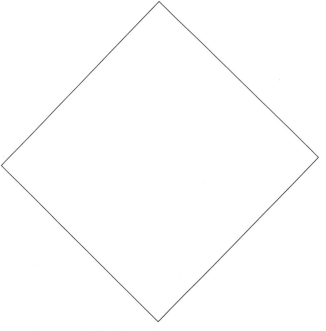

Diagram 4. The diamond.

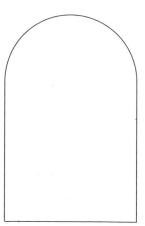

Diagram 5.
The arched rectangle.

Dividing the surface

The first impact that any work of art has upon the spectator is usually made by the arrangement of the main shapes on the surface and the divisions of the total space. Having considered which shape is most suitable for the idea you want to express, you need to think about how best to arrange or 'compose' your picture within the space. In any work the subject matter will be arranged in such a way as to impose some sort of basic division of the painting surface. What this is going to be is one of the first decisions to be made.

Taking a horizontal rectangle as the chosen shape (although many of the considerations that follow are equally applicable, whichever shape of surface you have chosen), the simplest division is by one line only. The most common way is a horizontal line right across the centre (as shown in diagram 6). This can be used by a skilful artist to good effect, but because each rectangle is equal, it is probably the least interesting of all arrangements. (Have a look at your own drawings and paintings and see if you have ever done this.)

The same rectangle, although still cut across by only one line as in diagram 7, is much more interesting when the two proportions are different. A division nearer the bottom of the painting gives you plenty of space for a fine sky or an interesting background. The foreground is reduced, so this division is ideal when the foreground presents you with several problems, since it allows you to cut out as much as possible.

The reverse of this (where the horizontal division is nearer the top of the painting, as shown in diagram 8), however, invites the artist to create an exciting foreground since it gives plenty of ground to cover to the horizon (assuming that you make the division coincide with the horizon). There is the opportunity to create a feeling of

Diagram 6. Divided by a central horizontal line.

Diagram 7. The low horizon.

Jacob van Ruisdael 'Landscape with Ruins' 1075 × 1440mm (43 × 57½in.). Van Ruisdael was a master of composition. In this painting the low horizon gives room for the billowing clouds in the sky, which disappears beyond and below the horizon.

great recession, and for the interesting development of things near to.

Many artists content themselves with a simple horizontal division of their surface, but more often than not they will make a vertical division of their compositions as well. The most obvious division, into four rectangles (as shown in diagram 9), can be made to work in the hands of a great artist, but is very dull otherwise. This arrangement demands that something very exciting is put into each rectangle to make the whole work. This can be a handicap. However, a vertical and horizontal division producing a juxtaposition of rectangles (diagram 10) makes a more interesting framework for a composition.

Perhaps your decisions as an artist in composing your work have so far been intuitive and this is right, but why not review your work and see if these simple suggestions may help to give greater interest to your compositions?

Diagram 8. The high horizon.

'Bathing Huts' 395 × 525mm (15½ × 21½in.). In this long composition the high horizon gives room for a full foreground. The study shows severe recession that takes the eye back in a rather lurching way into the design.

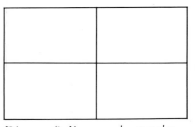

Diagram 9. Four equal rectangles.

'The Glebe Cottage' 405 × 550mm (16 × 22½in.). Here, the horizontal and repetitive lines of horizon, roof and walls are counterbalanced by the strong vertical through the chimney, gable and centre of the wall.

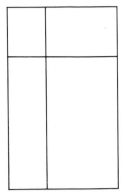

Diagram 10. Four rectangles of different sizes.

James McNeill Whistler 'Old Battersea Bridge: Nocturne in Blue and Gold' 679 × 508mm (26¾ × 20in.). It is not only to horizontal rectangles that the considerations on dividing the picture surface apply. In this upright painting, Whistler uses the deliberately heightened bridge to create the simple but dramatic vertical and horizontal divisions and force the eye upward to take in the firework display. Although he is ostensibly concerned with colour and tone to create the atmosphere, he needed space for the display on the right. He achieves this, and makes a satisfying composition, through the four unequal rectangles.

Harmonious proportion

Artists have always looked for both an ideal shape on which to work, and ideal proportions for that shape and several theories have evolved, two of which we will look at. The first is based on the relationship of squares and rectangles.

Construct a square ABCD (as shown in diagram 11). Produce the lines AB and DC. Using diagonal DB, describe an arc so that it intersects the produced line DC at F. From F draw a line at right angles to DF to intersect the produced line AB at E. The constructed rectangle AEFD has a harmonious relationship with the square ABCD. Repeat the procedure, using diagonal DE, to construct a further rectangle. This rectangle AHID has a harmonious relation with the square ABCD and the rectangle AEFD. This principle has long provided a rule-of-thumb method for artists seeking good proportion.

The second method of establishing fine proportion we will look at developed from the discovery of the Golden Mean, a direct result of the widespread interest in geometry and classical art in the Renaissance. The Golden Mean is also called the 'divine' proportion because while it is provable and demonstrable geometrically it cannot be resolved arithmetically, since it always results in an irrational fraction, .618 recurring.

Diagram 12 demonstrates how to discover the ideal proportion of a line AB (which could be the base or upright of a rectangle). Produce the line to C, so that CA is half the length of AB. From A draw a 90° vertical line AD the same length as AB. With the point of a pair of compasses at C describe an arc from D to intersect AB. The point of intersection G marks the Golden Mean of AB.

Diagram 13 is an extension of diagram 12. In it, the Golden Means of the rectangle ABCD are drawn in (in order not to make the diagram too unwieldy, the calculation lines of three sides, AB, BC, and CD only are shown). The points of intersection of the Golden Means W, X, Y and Z are also indicated.

It is interesting to look at how one of the great artists put the theory of the Golden Mean into practice. A study of the works of the English artist John Constable reveals that his paintings constructed and developed in the studio from studies made in the field always show his understanding of the Golden Mean. So familiar was he with this proportion that he used it instinctively when working on location and the knowledge never interfered with his spontaneity and freshness. His respect for the ideal or 'divine'

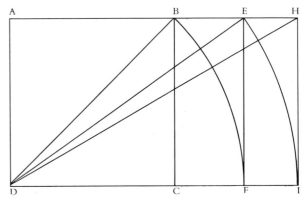

Diagram 11. The relationship of squares and rectangles.

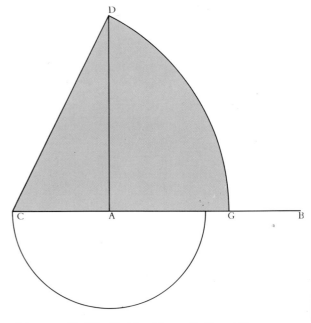

Diagram 12. The Golden Mean of a line AB.

proportion is evident from a detailed analysis of many of his works.

Constable regarded his painting 'The Cornfield', an upright design, as one of his best researched works, making studies beforehand of every detail, before building it into a fine satisfying painting. The parts did not appear in nature in the same positions as they do in the picture, since Constable has brought Dedham Church into view, in the background. The Golden Means have been calculated along with the main directional lines. It becomes very obvious that intersecting lines, whether within the main picture area or on the edges, assume a greater importance than disconnected lines which do not touch other lines or the edges of the picture. It is usually on these intersections that centres of interest are placed to great effect; those placed on the intersections of the Golden Means have the greatest effect. Try this exercise yourself with a reproduction of a great painting.

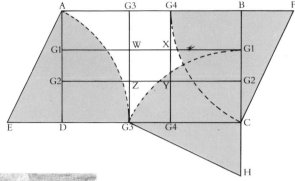

Above: Diagram 13. The Golden Means of a horizontal rectangle. These are found by taking each of the sides of the rectangle and determining its Golden Mean, as shown in diagram 12.

John Constable 'The Cornfield' 1429 × 1219mm (56¼ × 48in.). This painting shows Constable's understanding of the Golden Mean. The overlaid lines G1, G2, G3 and G4 mark the main Golden Sections, and it is along these lines that Constable placed his major points of interest, including the dog. The church, placed on an intersection of two of these lines has even greater prominence. The boy in the bottom left of the picture is exactly at the intersections of the Golden Sections of that rectangle: G5, G6, G7 and G8.

Creating a composition

Composition also involves arranging shapes within your picture area. Excited by a knowledge of proportion and shape it is tempting to be over-ambitious and use far too great a variety of shape within your composition. When three simple shapes, such as a triangle, rhomboid and circle, are placed separately in a composition or overlap each other (as shown in diagram 14), the viewer can identify each shape, read what it is and enjoy the interplay. The addition of one more shape, particularly an irregular one as shown in diagram 15, obscures their identities, however, and while the design may still hold up it would require only one more shape to create incoherence or confusion.

The last two points to consider here are, firstly, that a horizontal shape with easy flowing directional lines gives a sense of passivity or tranquillity, whereas strongly opposed lines and lines not parallel to the edges convey a sense of agitation, dynamism, or activity. Secondly, directional lines leading into corners take the viewer's eye out of the design. Avoid them unless you wish to create an impression of explosion.

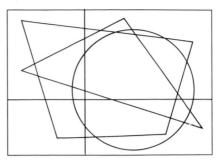

Diagram 14. Three shapes are readable.

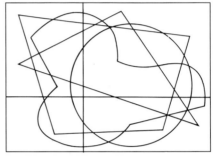

Diagram 15. One more is confusing.

PROVING MOUNTS (MATS)

Proving mounts are indispensable when designing a drawing or painting. Cut two L shapes from a piece of card (as shown in diagram 16). Gather all the work you have so far done, including those sketches you thought insignificant, and place the mounts around them. Then adjust the sizes and shape, taking pieces out of the picture, making square compositions long and upright from square. You may find, for instance, that instead of the horizon dividing your composition across the middle it looks much more interesting with less sky or even very little foreground.

Keep these proving mounts handy while composing your pictures – they will be of great assistance.

Viewing frames are also useful. Make three from dark-faced card – the first with a rectangular aperture of the proportions 3:5, based on the Golden Mean; the second with a square aperture

J.M.W. Turner 'The Evening Star' 900 × 1200mm (36 × 48in.). Although unfinished, this painting expresses a great sense of tranquillity. The equilibrium of the design creates a very still atmosphere.

Paolo Uccello 'Battle of San Romano'(detail) 1790 × 2950mm (71½ × 126in.). In this dynamic design, the conflicting angles of the lances and juxtapositions of each feature lead the eye out of the canvas.

3:3; and the third with a rectangular aperture of the proportions 3:4¼ based lengthwise on the diagonal of the square.

Practice is necessary to use viewing frames successfully; they can, however, be invaluable in helping you create a composition.

Close one eye and hold the frame a few centimetres from your open eye, then move it away until it is at arm's length. You will notice that the closer it is to the eye the greater the breadth of view you have through it, and the further away it is from your eye the narrower and more restricted is the view. Cut paper or prepare boards on which you are going to work to exactly the same proportions, for example, 30 × 50cm (12 × 20in.), 30 × 30cm (12 × 12in.) and 30 × 43cm (12 × 17in.). Find interesting still lifes or views from your window, and move your viewing frame until you see through the aperture how much you wish to draw. Then arrange the shapes as you see them through your viewing frame. (At this stage, work only in line. Don't try to add a third dimension.) Try moving your viewpoint lower or higher, and make drawings from these positions. Immediately your compositions will take on greater originality, and you will see shapes more clearly and use them more effectively than before.

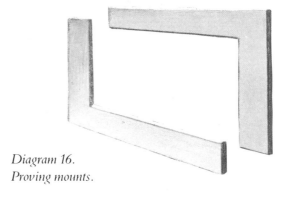

Diagram 16.
Proving mounts.

2 Approaching perspective

In chapter 1, we looked at the linear aspect of composition, although we all know that gradations of tone of light to dark from white to black will add to the drama of fine composition. We are also aware, however, that we expect this flat composition – the two-dimensional structure of the surface – to be supported by an understandable structure in the third dimension. This can be achieved by tonal changes, by the use of colour or by an awareness of the principles of perspective. Perspective exists all around us – vanishing points, for example, can be traced from buildings and your eye level is a constant. Before we turn to the principles of perspective, and how they are applied in drawing and painting, however, it is necessary to become familiar with the technical terms that are used in dealing with perspective. These are not purely academic but have a practical value for the artist because they relate to and clarify the visual assumptions we make about the world around us.

Diagram 17. In this book, the blue line is the eye level.

Key terms

Almost everyone who has written about perspective, or who has taught it, has invented their own terms for the different elements. Some are widely used and well known, but others seem less familiar. To prevent confusion for those with some knowledge of perspective, and to establish these elements for those who are coming to it fresh, here is a list of the terms that I shall be using, together with definitions and alternatives you may meet elsewhere. The abbreviations are those used throughout the rest of this book.

Angle of Incidence   The angle formed between a ray of light as it strikes an object and the object's surface.

Angle of Reflection   The angle between a ray of light and the surface of an object as it bounces off that object. It equals the angle of incidence.

Centre of Vision – CV   Also termed Central Vanishing Point (CVP), Point of Sight (PS), Principal Vanishing Point (PVP). This is the nearest point on the picture plane (see below)

opposite your eye. It is found at the intersection of the lines of sight and eye level. Imagine that you are looking down the sights of a rifle held horizontally; the point of aim would be the centre of vision.

Elevation   A drawing of what you would see if you were standing directly in front of the subject.

Eye – E (black bullet)   Sometimes termed the Spectator (S) or Viewer (V). This is the point from which your eye views the subject.

Eye Level – EL (blue line)   This is a complete horizontal circle at your eye level as you turn your head or the horizon if you are at sea level. Everything in perspective is related to this line.

Ground Line – GL   A measuring line, this is a line running along the ground parallel to the eye level. A measured scale can be marked on it and projected back to the CV or VPs to give lateral measurements.

Ground Plane – GP   An imaginary horizontal flat extension of the ground on which you stand, it extends forwards from your feet to the eye level on the picture plane.

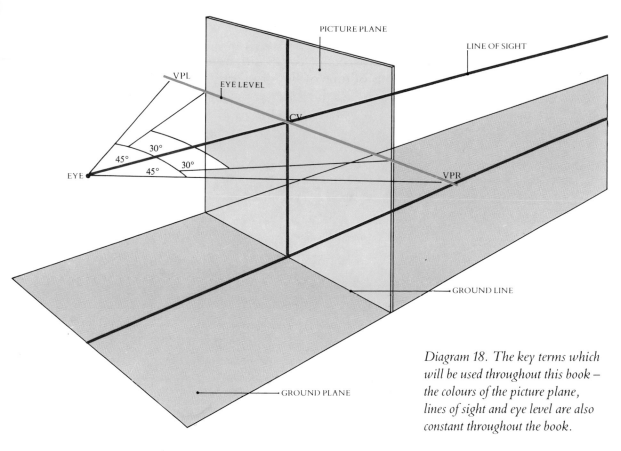

Diagram 18. The key terms which will be used throughout this book – the colours of the picture plane, lines of sight and eye level are also constant throughout the book.

Horizon – H   In mountainous or hilly country it is the dividing line between sky and land and may be well above the eye level (or below in three-point perspective).

Line of Sight – LS (red lines)   Also termed Distance Line (DL). This is the line from the eye to the picture plane and which intersects it at 90°. Measuring it establishes the distance you are from the picture plane.

Parallels of Perspective   The term Vanishing Parallels (VP) is also used. These are lines seen on a plan as parallel, but in perspective they appear to converge at a point on the eye level at infinity.

Picture Plane – PP (solid blue)   This is an imaginary vertical plane at right angles to the line of sight upon which a drawing or painting is drafted. It can be regarded as the surface of your board or canvas. To help understand it, think of it

as a vertical sheet of clear glass at a short distance from you, through which you view your subject. What is seen on the picture plane is shaped by two factors: the height that the eye is from the ground line and the distance the subject is from the eye. The distance between eye and subject is usually equal to the greater dimension of your picture.

Plan   A drawing of something done as if you were looking at it from directly above.

Trace Lines   Lines which plot one point on a form to another, or the path of a shadow on an object on the ground plane or across the object.

Vanishing Points – VP   Also termed Distance Points (DP). These are points on the eye level on either side of the centre of vision to which parallel lines going away from you converge and appear to vanish. They can be extended to infinity to left and right – known as vanishing point left (VPL) and vanishing point right (VPR). While for your subject the natural vanishing points may occur on or about the extremes of your board, it is likely that they may be some distance outside the edges. A piece of card pinned along the foot of the board can be fixed at an inclined angle, and two lines from a central point at the bottom drawn upwards in the approximate directions of the vanishing points as shown in diagram 19. This is a very inaccurate guide, but can be of use if you extend the lines in your imagination or point in the appropriate directions. You can persuade people looking at your work to stand back from the picture to the position from which you want it to be seen by placing your vanishing points further away from the edges of the painting.

Diagram 19. Determining vanishing points.

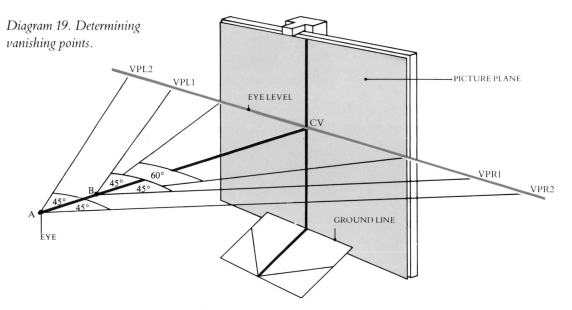

How we see

Lines in a composition that slope inwards away from the edge of the picture immediately create the illusion of depth. In diagram 20 in real life the lines represented by AB and CD are assumed to be the same length, but AB appears further away than CD. On a similar assumption the points labelled E appear further away than F. This illusion is heightened by the line XY which we visually assume is a distant horizon. This diagram could be a drawing on a flat vertical wall.

In diagram 21 a similar visual assumption is made. AB appears much nearer than CD and EF. We tend to assume that each line is really the same height, and that the smaller ones are further away. This time XY leaves us in less doubt that it is a distant horizon. The three figures in diagram 22 are even more compelling in the way they assume their positions in space. We immediately think that figure C is nearest and A and B further away.

Let us now look at *how* these 'optical illusions' happen. Close one eye, then stand or sit upright

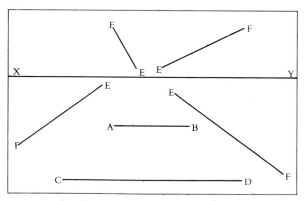

Diagram 20. We assume CD is nearer than AB.

and fix your gaze on a spot straight in front, level with your eye. Raise and extend both your arms and hands in front of you, then open your arms until you can no longer see your hands with any definition. Most people open their arms to about 60° before being unable to see the hands in clear focus, so the average 'cone of vision' is taken to be 60°. Perspective, in theory, does not work if both your eyes are open.

Imagine you are looking through a pane of glass at two identical vertical pegs in the ground outside as shown in diagram 23. The rays of light from the pegs converge on the eye. The rays from the one furthest away have converged much more than the nearer one so the further peg will appear smaller on the glass pane, and correspondingly the nearer peg will appear larger and below the one further away. Diagram 24 shows two lengths of timber lying on the ground first in plan view and then seen through a pane of glass. The lines of sight converging on the eye show the piece of timber GH appearing much shorter than EF where they pass through the glass.

Now imagine that the pane of glass you have been looking through is a piece of paper or board. The way in which your eyes have perceived the lengths of timber through the glass is the way you should draw them, measuring off their heights and lengths on to the paper.

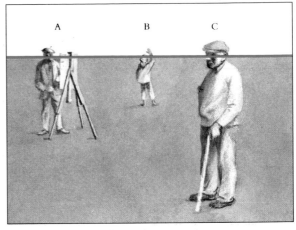

Diagram 22. C is obviously nearer than A or B.

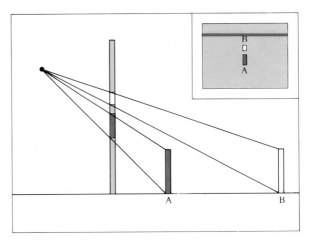

Diagram 23. The farther peg looks shorter.

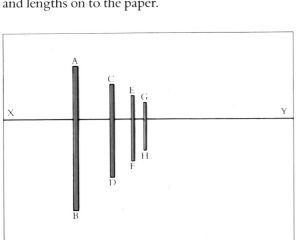

Diagram 21. We assume AB is nearer than CD.

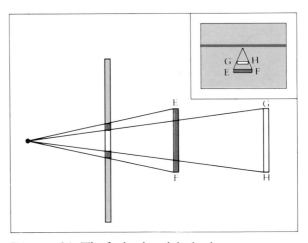

Diagram 24. The farther length looks shorter.

A classic example of these principles put into practice is the drawing of parallel railway lines disappearing into the distance (as shown in diagram 25). The tracks get smaller and closer together as they recede until the lines meet at a point on the horizon on the eye level – at infinity.

Left: Diagram 25. The tracks get smaller and closer together as they recede.

Aids to drawing

Over the years, artists, illustrators and draughtsmen have developed various ways to help them represent accurately what they see in front of them. These 'aids' to drawing, and you should remember that they are only that (not rules to follow slavishly or devices you must buy or make), vary from the simple and familiar to the more mechanical and technical. You may, however, find some of them very useful.

Measuring by eye with a pencil

A simple means of estimating and comparing proportions, particularly vertical and horizontal distances, is by using a pencil as a measure. Select the object you wish to use as a yardstick for your drawing, then hold your pencil out, making sure your arm is fully extended. Align the top of the pencil with the top of the object and your finger with the bottom (as shown in diagram 26). This 'measurement' will allow you to estimate the other objects in proportion. Ensure when

measuring depths that the pencil is absolutely vertical. When estimating pitch or measuring horizontally, the pencil has to be at right angles to your line of vision. When estimating an angle, start with the pencil horizontal, then rotate it until it lies along the line. This will establish the angle.

Sight size

Working 'sight size' is a useful technique to employ. Diagram 27 shows how this system would work when tackling a 'still life' of a cube on a small table. If you are right-handed, you will need to look round the left side of the drawing board so that your drawing hand does not cross the lines of sight and obscure your vision. With the board vertical and one eye closed, move your head slightly to left and right so that the board's edge can be used as a plumb line to determine the varying heights of each part of the objects, and mark these points on the edge of the board. This is particularly useful when figure drawing, but can also be used to good effect when drawing a landscape or, as here, a still life. This is a time-honoured method, proved by the ticks to be seen down the edge of many a master's drawing, indicating he was drawing sight size.

We perceive objects in a plane which is at right angles to our line of vision. In the case of looking straight ahead the plane is vertical, as if it were a sheet of glass suspended in front of us. However, when you are drawing your board may be on your knees or on a sloping easel, so that you will have to look down; the tendency, nevertheless, is still to

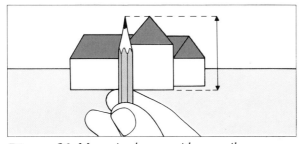

Diagram 26. Measuring by eye with a pencil.

visualize the vertical plane before your eye. To 'translate' this vertical image to a board at an angle requires complex mental adjustments of proportion. There is a danger that you may overadjust, making the bottom half of what you are drawing much too big. If you are a beginner, it is probably easier to use a vertical board until you have had more practice and are more proficient.

The obvious exception to using a vertical board is when drawing a horizontal subject, say a landscape-shaped still life or, indeed, a real landscape. It is then much easier to look over the top (as shown in diagram 28). Hold the board horizontally beneath your subject, but close up against it, with one eye closed. Then, with your free hand, tick off the widths of the details of your subject along the top edge of your paper.

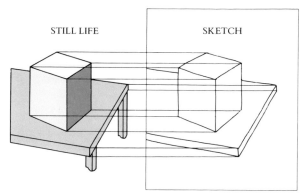

Diagram 27. Working sight size.

Your drawings might at first appear stilted or stiff using these methods; however, with practice the techniques will become instinctive and no longer inhibit your style.

Diagram 28. The principle of working sight size applied to a landscape.

Mechanical aids

Albrecht Dürer used a drawing frame with a rather elaborate mechanism. The eyepiece could be moved laterally with a thread and turnbuckle, and backwards or forwards, keeping it square with the table top. The glazed frame was also held vertically. A simpler version can be constructed with a picture frame, without its backing but with its glass, clamped on to a table. The critical part of this piece of equipment is the eyepiece. It must be steady for you to be able to produce accurate results. Position the frame and eyepiece so your arm and hand holding a brush loaded with permanent white gouache colour, or a chinagraph pencil (china marker), can reach the glass comfortably (this may take practice).

You will find that, as one eye is closed, it will, at first, be difficult to judge the distance your hand is from the glass. You then draw what you see on to the framed glass. Once the image has been completed, it can be traced off on to thin paper, giving you precise angles, shape and proportion for your drawing.

There are other mechanical aids to drawing, such as the Camera Obscura, which basically consists of a box with a magnifying lens. This produces an upside-down image on a screen which can then be traced off. A Camera Ottica is similar to a Camera Obscura but since it has a mirror inside, it rights the image produced by the lens; it does take some experimentation to make it work. Many eighteenth-century artists, including the great Venetian master Canaletto, are believed to have used such an instrument extensively. Such mechanical aids are fun to make and use, but are no real substitute for the judgements of your eye. Similarly a camera, although it can be a useful tool and reminder, and is to some people a source of inspiration, cannot give you the reasoned sensitivity to space that can be developed by keen observation and expressed by a sound understanding of perspective.

This illustration reproduced from Underweyssung der Messung, *first published in 1525, shows Albrecht Dürer's drawing frame in use. The artist moves the eyepiece back and forth until he can see through the glass as much or as little of his subject (here a figure) as he wishes to paint or draw. He can then trace the outline on to the glass. If he wants to paint a picture from this, he simply transfers the tracing on to his canvas.*

3 Principles of perspective

We now understand how converging rays make us see objects that we know to be the same size as varying sizes because of the different distances they are from the eye. The next step is to know how by applying the rules of perspective these variations can be expressed and appreciated intelligently in your drawings and paintings. You will probably find it useful to keep referring to the definitions of terms on pages 20–2, initially at least.

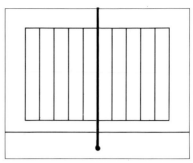

Diagram 29. Plan of floorboards.

Parallel perspective

Parallel perspective is employed when one side of what is facing you is parallel to the picture plane.

Take a plan view of floorboards, seen from above. As diagram 29 shows, they are all parallel and recede, and they are also all equal in width. When viewed on the picture plane, however (diagram 30), they converge and if extended meet at one point on the eye level which is at the viewer's centre of vision. As they are equal in width, their width measurements can be marked along the ground line at the foot of the picture plane. At any other point in their length the relative measurement of any board's width will be as it would be seen in perspective.

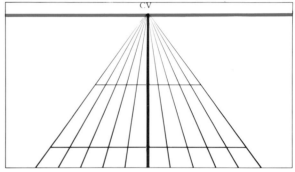

Diagram 30. On the PP, the boards converge.

The position of the viewer alters the appearance of the floorboards (as shown in diagrams 31 and 32). However, there is a limit as to how far you can move to right or left and still employ the rules of parallel perspective. As soon as you have to turn your head to see the whole object then you must use the rules of oblique perspective (see pages 35–8). At this stage we can summarize the first rules of parallel perspective:

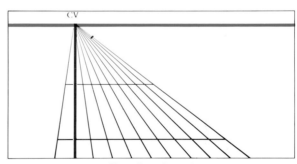

Diagram 31. View of boards to the right.

1 Parallel lines receding from the eye appear to converge and meet at a point at infinity. If these lines are in a horizontal plane and parallel to the line of sight, that point at which they meet is the centre of vision and is on the eye level.
2 Lines which are parallel to the picture plane, that is at right angles to the line of sight, have no vanishing point.

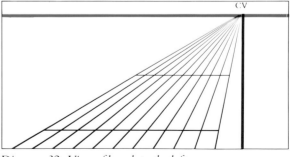

Diagram 32. View of boards to the left.

DRAWING AN INTERIOR

Having constructed a floor following the rules of parallel perspective, it is a very simple procedure to erect a vertical to any size you like at each corner and create an interior. Always start your drawings by establishing an eye level and a centre of vision. All the vanishing lines to the centre of vision are then fairly simple to plot.

The only new feature in the drawing below is the door ajar. Both the top and bottom of the door, since they are parallel, will vanish to a point on the eye level to the left of the CV. Once you have decided how far open you want the door to be, the vanishing lines of the top and the bottom can then be determined.

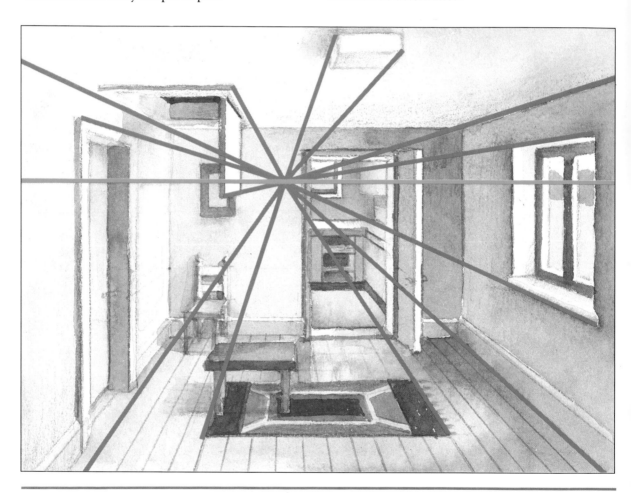

Using diagonals

It is useful to know how to find the centre of a rectangle or square whether in plan view or perspective. This is done by simply drawing in the diagonals. You will notice from the elevation of diagram 33 that the perspective centre makes the back half of square ABFE narrower than the front half EFCD. The diagonals of the square have their common vanishing point on the eye level outside the area of the picture plane. The real advantage of constructing these diagonals is that they allow you to measure the depth of each rectangle in

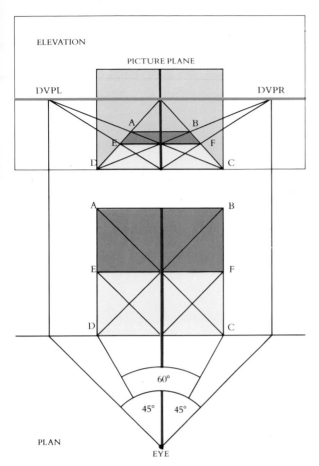

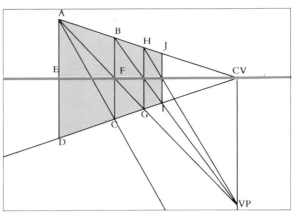

Diagram 34. Using diagonals to establish depth.

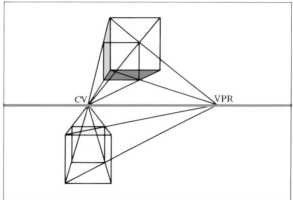

Diagram 33. The centre of a square, plan and elevation.

Diagram 35. Cubes above and below the eye level.

perspective, without resort to holding your pencil at arm's length, when you are drawing from objects or constructing forms from imagination or memory. In this way, you can achieve a convincing feeling of depth in your drawings and paintings.

It is not just horizontal distances that can be measured. It is also possible to measure the equal spaces between verticals in perspective (suppose, for example, you wanted to draw a receding row of vertical posts alongside a flat, straight road as in diagram 34). Decide where you want your first two posts to be. Then, establish a diagonal VP for the space between the posts, this will be immediately below the centre of vision. The diagonal AC produced will make a very long line

before it intersects a vertical dropped from the CV. Lack of space may make it impractical. A diagonal dropped through the eye level (E to CV), however, will work just as well. AF produced to meet a vertical dropped from the CV gives you your VP and the base of your third post (G). A vertical from G to H is your third post. A line from your VP to B gives the base of your fourth post (I) and so on.

Cubic shapes above and below the eye level can also be constructed by using diagonals (you may need the principles in order to put clouds in one of your pictures). A diagonal to the VPR in diagram 35 tells you where the back of the cube should be placed. The backs and faces are, obviously, drawn in parallel perspective.

A SIMPLE COMPOSITION

You should now be able to make very interesting drawings using simple parallel perspective and diagonal parallels. Establish your eye level, then decide compositionally what you want to appear facing you (here the ends of the buildings). Draw those in (here, since all the roofs are parallel, their slopes are also parallel). Diagonals are used here to establish the spacing of the fence posts on the right, although they too recede to the CV. The fence posts on the left are parallel to the PP, so don't recede.

Calculating depth

The calculation of depth (that is, where the 'back' of the room should be placed, or how far away the next fence post should be) of a shape in perspective initially seems a problem. If you are working on sight, you can measure it with your eye, or if in doubt with a vertically held pencil. If you can confine the shape you are drawing in a square or rectangle, the diagonal vanishing points can be fixed and depths established in that way. A simple way when working in the studio or to gain

a clear understanding is to make a plan as in diagram 36. This shows how a shape ABCD behind the picture plane and ground line can be accurately placed. The lines of sight intersecting the picture plane establish the widths of the back of the shape. When the width of the back is dropped vertically on to the vanishing parallels, you can establish the precise depth of the square.

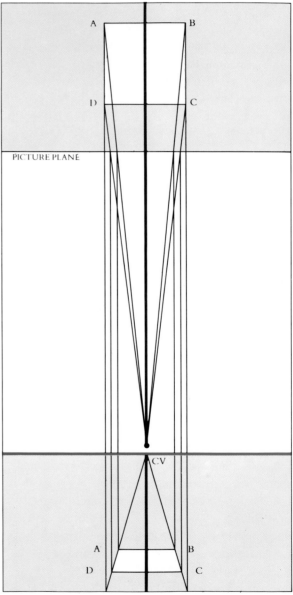

Diagram 36. A plan to enable you to calculate depth.

Placing figures in a landscape

A common problem is to depict people scattered on a flat surface and to establish their relative sizes. Draw a measuring line vertically on the left side of your board. In diagram 37, our artist standing with his sketch pad is 1.8m (6ft) tall and the other seated artist is 1.1m (3ft 6in.) high. These two measurements are projected back to the centre of vision and they represent a 1.8m (6ft) and 1.1m (3ft 6in.) height from the ground for the whole depth of the drawing. By carrying horizontals to left or right the whole area is covered by these measurements. The figures are placed between those lines where they compositionally fit.

Diagram 37. Relative heights of figures in a landscape.

A more common problem, and one over which students and experienced artists stumble, is how to place a figure or an object accurately in front of the picture plane (without making it appear that they are standing in a trench or on a chair).

Diagram 38 illustrates what we see with a normal eye level at 1.5m (5ft) from the ground. This is fixed by a measuring line, once again up the left-hand side of the picture plane. This time the receding lines on the ground have been extended forward of the picture plane as well as back to the centre of vision. From this, it is clear how much of the figures in front of the picture plane should logically be included in the composition.

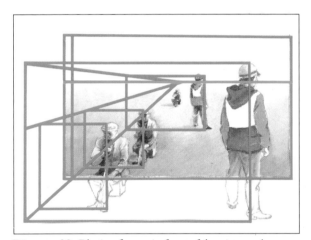

Diagram 38. Placing figures in front of the picture plane.

Inclined and declined planes

Many artists have used inclines and declines in their compositions to create an almost giddy feeling of recession in their designs. The principles involved in creating inclines and declines are the same as those used with a flat horizontal plane with the exception that if the vanishing points are parallel to the horizontal plane, they will appear immediately above or below the centre of vision on which parallel receding lines will converge.

Normally you would not have to calculate the angle of slope but would rely on the sureness of your eye viewing the subject. However, in a composition in the studio, the angle may well

'Holiday Chalet'. An example of inclined planes.

have as much to do with your compositional need for a line going in that direction as the precise angle of slope.

Diagram 39 shows three shapes A, B and C. All are the same width, and in parallel perspective all would recede to the CV. However, if you wanted A to slope downwards and C to slope up, you have to establish vanishing points immediately above and below the CV. The descending slope from A to D in this diagram from the position of the decline vanishing point (VPD) shows how little of this plane would be seen.

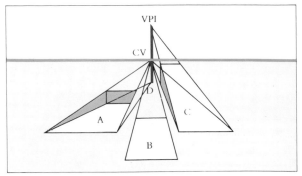

Diagram 39. Establishing vanishing points for slopes.

Slopes can be established by incline and decline VPs. In diagram 40, the straight road first runs level (A) then slopes down (section B). The vanishing point for the decline (VPD) is indicated. The road then runs level again (section C). This section vanishes at the CV. The road then ascends gently (section D) and the vanishing point for the incline (VPI) is indicated. Finally the road levels off and disappears to the centre of vision at the eye level. The fencing and wall slope at the same angle as the road, and because they are parallel to it, their vanishing points coincide.

Roofs, of course, are inclined planes and where they appear in recession (roofs A, C and D in diagram 41), they will have an incline vanishing point above the CV. The slopes of roofs B and E will not have vanishing points as they are parallel to the ground line and picture plane.

'Northern Suburb' 375 × 612mm (15 × 24½in.). Receding roofs create a convincing feeling of space.

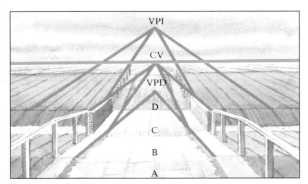

Diagram 40. How to draw a sloping road.

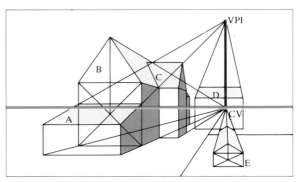

Diagram 41. Establishing VPs for roofs.

A STREET SCENE

You now have almost all the knowledge you need in order to be able to create a design with a descending and ascending road in recession, lined by buildings. There are two further points to understand.

Firstly, houses nearly always appear to go down in steps. Secondly, roofs, doors, windowsills and lintels are usually horizontal and so vanish to the CV, not the VPD. Establish your eye level and centre of vision, then decide how much of a decline you want in your street. Decide on a decline vanishing point, immediately below the CV. The tops and bottoms of the houses on the slope will vanish to the VPD.

Drawing circles and ellipses

We know that circles fit into squares and from diagram 33 we know how to draw a square in perspective. Circles or ellipses always have to be constructed in parallel perspective. Diagram 42 shows how ellipses can be constructed. Draw a square in perspective, and draw in the diagonals. Draw the front half of a circle from A to B freehand, touching C. Lines to the CV through where the half circle crosses the diagonals will give you the points through which to draw the back half of the circle.

There is one important point to remember if you are using this knowledge of ellipses to draw cylinders. You will remember from diagram 33 that the perspective centre of a square made the front half look bigger than the back. This is also, obviously, true of the centre line of an ellipse – it will make the back look smaller than the front. For this reason, you do not find the width of a cylinder by dropping verticals from the extremities of the perspective centre line, but from the widest portion of the ellipse. This is shown in diagram 43. The contours or edges that you would see are the lines XY and WZ.

When you are drawing cylindrical objects, it is better at the start to draw the whole ellipse, although only a portion of it may be seen. In this way the smooth rhythm of a compressed circle is best obtained. When you are satisfied with your shapes, erase those lines you don't need.

Once you have mastered drawing ellipses, all sorts of round and curved items – bicycles, pots, cups and glasses – can be included with effect in your compositions.

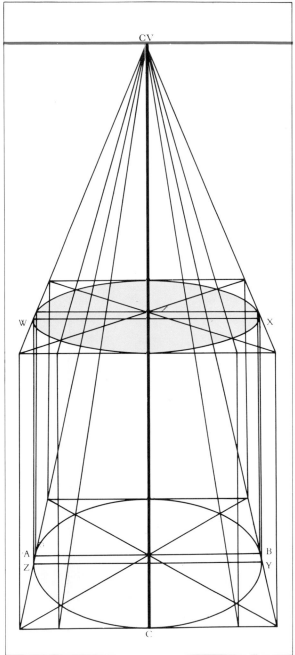

Diagram 43. Drawing a cylinder.

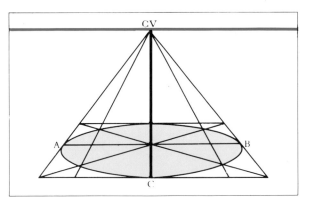

Diagram 42. Drawing a circle in perspective.

Oblique perspective

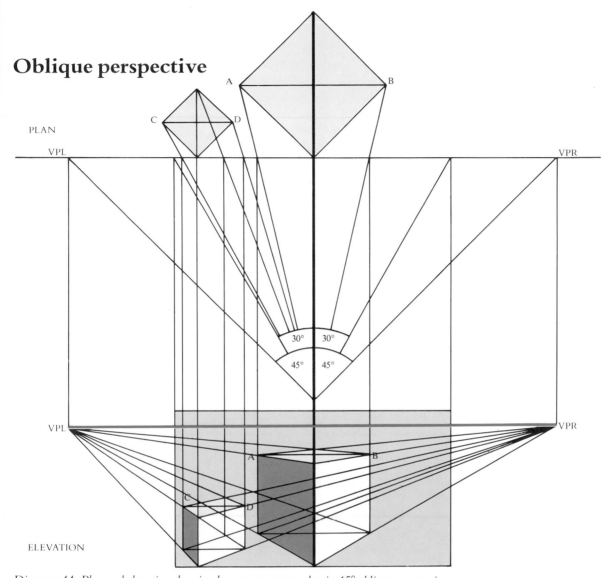

PLAN

ELEVATION

Diagram 44. Plan and elevation showing how to construct cubes in 45° oblique perspective.

A moment's observation reveals that objects in nature rarely oblige by lying parallel and at right angles to the eye level. They are nearly always at angles to it. Rules of perspective still govern these random dispositions, however, and, when applied, they help artists to create convincing form and space, and make a forceful contribution to composing a picture.

We have seen (pages 28-30) that by creating a 45° angle on either side of the line of vision vanishing points can be located that are in fact the points to which diagonals of squares in the design

converge. This gives a geometrically calculated and convincing depth. Vanishing points are not necessarily at this 45° angle from the line of sight, but perspective (rather like some games) works well if you make rules from convenient assumptions. A useful set of rules can also be assumed if a 60°/30° perspective is used. They again will allow you to establish relative depths coherently and yet they will produce a totally different viewpoint and appearance.

Diagram 44 is similar to diagram 36 on page 30. It shows a 45° perspective from a top plan projection and an elevation. It is very unusual for a creative artist to use a projection like this and I wouldn't recommend that you do either, but it does help you to understand how the lengths of the sides of the two squares are seen on the picture plane by the lines of sight passing through it, to the eye. These sizes projected down to the elevation form the basis for constructing the cubes. The size of the picture is governed by the 60° cone of vision.

One important point to notice is that where the edges of the squares are parallel to the vanishing parallels, the diagonals of each square AB and CD are parallel to the picture plane, that is, they are horizontal. The second point to notice is that the closer you get to the edges of the 60° field of

vision, the more distorted the cube appears. Outside that field of vision objects become progressively more distorted as the smaller cube illustrates. This looks more like a rectangular attaché case than a cube (to have avoided drawing it like this, you would have to have been standing further away). Perspective, then, has its limitations. As an artist, you must understand and either compensate for, or decide to exploit, these limitations.

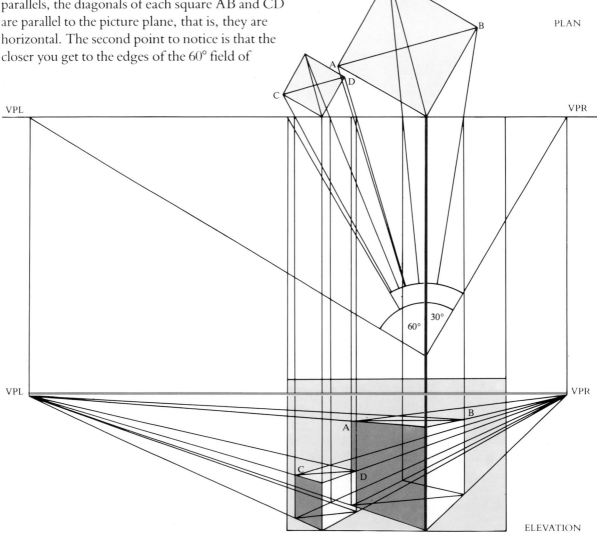

Diagram 45. The same cubes in 60°/30° perspective.

Diagram 45 demonstrates what happens to these cubes in 60°/30° perspective. The differences are obvious. Firstly, far more of the near side of the cubes is visible. Secondly, the vanishing parallels are again parallel to the sides of the squares, but these are more oblique to the eye level and picture plane than they were in 45° perspective. Also, the distortion of the smaller cube does not look so great due to the greater distance it is from the VPL. Finally, you can see that the diagonals of the cubes are not parallel to the picture plane or to eye level.

Diagrams 46 and 47 show these points in a 'real' situation. The first uses a high eye level and is drawn in 45° perspective. We are viewing the buildings from a distance, so no distortion occurs.

Gable ends and fronts are equally seen. In the second, although the centre of vision is in almost the same place, the buildings are angled at 60°/30°. Their structure is still right-angled but because of the acute angle of vision we can see the front more fully and the gable ends less so. The gap between the buildings has also disappeared and the sharper angles give a less symmetrical look to the group than in the 45° perspective drawing.

Depth in oblique perspective

As we saw in the section on parallel perspective, ascertaining convincing depths in perspective, at first, seems difficult. There are many ways of doing this (as discussed on pages 28–30), and here ways to establish depth in oblique perspective are shown. The square WXYZ in diagram 48 has been constructed in 45° perspective, its depth established by the diagonal XZ. The diamond-shaped square ABCD is simply put into WXYZ, its diagonal corresponding with the perspective centre of WXYZ and parallel to the eye level.

Occasionally, however, you will want to establish the depth of a square that is less conveniently angled to your line of sight and eye level. The square ABCD in diagram 49 is more typical of the kind of problem you will find! Draw WXYZ in as a guide. From points A and C, draw lines parallel to the sides of the square XY and WZ, then draw in the diagonal of WXYZ (ZX).

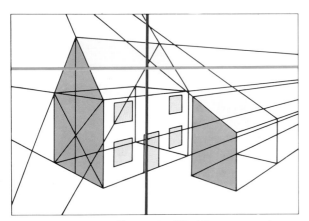

Diagram 46. View of houses in 45° oblique perspective.

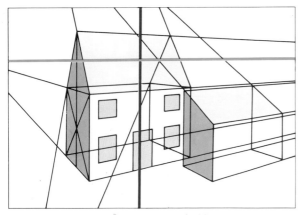

Diagram 47. The houses in 60°/30° oblique perspective.

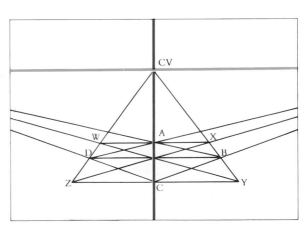

Diagram 48. Depth of a square in 45° oblique perspective.

From the points where these lines AE and CF intersect the diagonal (G and H) draw horizontals to WZ and XY to create the small interior squares FXBG and DHEZ. This can now be drafted into WXYZ which in diagram 50 has been constructed in parallel perspective. The lines EA and CF (measured along the foot of square WXYZ) recede. From the intersection of EA and CF with the diagonal XZ, the position of D and B can be ascertained. The square ABCD can then be constructed. DA and CB converge and if produced can be checked for accuracy. They meet on the eye level at VP.

This knowledge of oblique perspective should now enable you to create an interesting composition. Always decide first on an eye level

and place your vanishing points and centre of vision where you wish them to be. A simple rule of thumb if you wish to be accurate is, when using 45° perspective, to make your vanishing points equal distances from the centre of vision. The further apart you place them, the further away you are from your picture plane. If you are using 30°/60° perspective, the 60° vanishing point is roughly three times further from the centre of vision than the 30° vanishing point is. Although this is not a strictly accurate figure, it is a reasonable working estimate, and if you apply it you will find that it will generally produce convincing drawings.

Inclines and declines
Inclined and declined planes were discussed on pages 31–2. A knowledge of oblique perspective, however, enables a more convincing use of inclines and declines. Diagram 51 illustrates the way they could appear in a small harbour. Since this is in 45° oblique perspective, the right and left vanishing points are equal distances from the centre of vision on each side. The VPs are a long way outside the picture plane to left and right, indicating that the artist was standing well back. Also, because this is a sea view, the eye level is also the horizon. The ramps or hards incline and decline and their vanishing points lie immediately above and below the right-hand vanishing point.

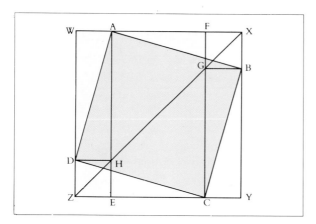

Diagram 49. An inconveniently angled square.

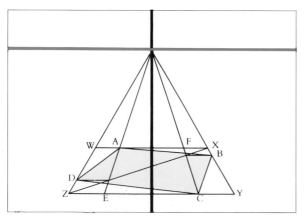

Diagram 50. The same square in plan view.

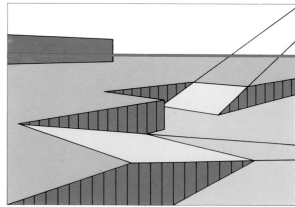

Diagram 51. Inclines and declines in oblique perspective.

A KITCHEN SCENE

This illustration is a very simplified version of the corner of a kitchen projected in 30°/60° perspective, and you now have all the knowledge you need in order to draw something like this. As already stated it was necessary to establish the eye level, the centre of vision and the 30° vanishing point on the left and the 60° vanishing point to the right. Such drawings can be put together even away from the subject without difficulty, if each point is established and logically constructed.

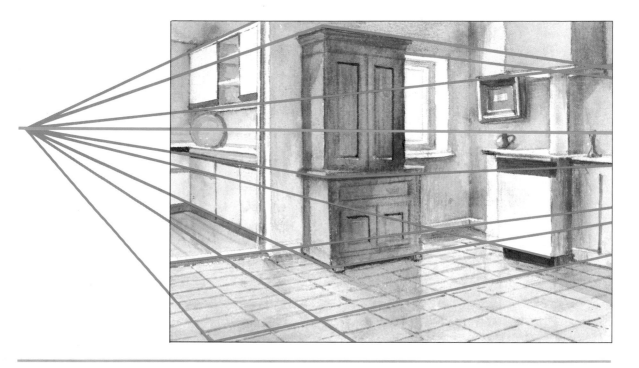

'Dinghies on the Hard' 473 × 640mm (19 × 25½in.). The almost random ridges along the inclined slopes – formed by planks being set on the still wet concrete – contribute to a powerful impression of recession. The boats, under covers, create a lateral rocking rhythm, but do not cut the composition in two because the lines of the foreground extend upwards to the top of the picture through the masts.

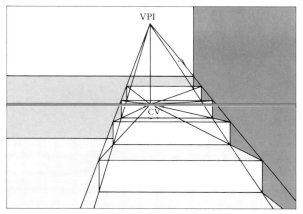

Diagram 52. Stairs in parallel perspective from the side.

Stairs

The perspective of stairs and of steps, rather like that of the roofs of buildings, is based on the presence of inclined and declined planes. Diagram 52 shows a series of stairs seen from the side and in parallel perspective. The lines connecting the treads (AB and CD) are parallel to EF and GH, although due to the recession of the stair treads,

'Mortlake Steps' 398 × 440mm (16 × 17½in.). Here, bank, causeway, wall and steps all contribute to recession.

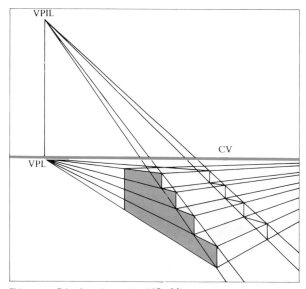

Diagram 53. Stairs, seen from in front.

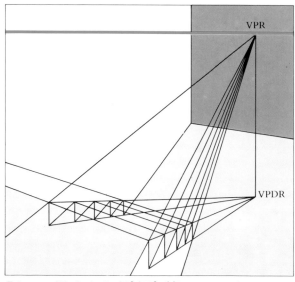

Diagram 54. A staircase in 45° oblique perspective.

Diagram 55. Stairs in 30°/60° oblique perspective.

EF and GH are much closer than AB and CD. In stairs viewed from the front and in parallel perspective, however, these tread lines all converge on the VPI (incline), which is immediately above the CV (diagram 53).

In a staircase seen in 45° oblique perspective (diagram 54), the tread lines converge on the VPI left which is immediately above the VP left. As in diagram 52, the lines connecting the front treads are farther apart than those connecting the rear.

Normally, we view stairs in very sharp perspective when we are about to go down them, as we are not only looking straight down from above, but have the added height of our own bodies. The visual effect of this is shown clearly in the 30°/60° projection of diagram 55.

AN ARRANGEMENT OF STAIRS

A complex and fanciful arrangement of stairs, like this one, should now be within your capabilities. These are in a 30°/60° projection. Establish your eye level, and decide where you want the stairs to come into your drawing. Next decide on the height of your stairs. Indicate the slopes of the stairs by deciding on the VPI and VPD. Constructing the arrangement should not now present you with any problems if you follow the preceding principles.

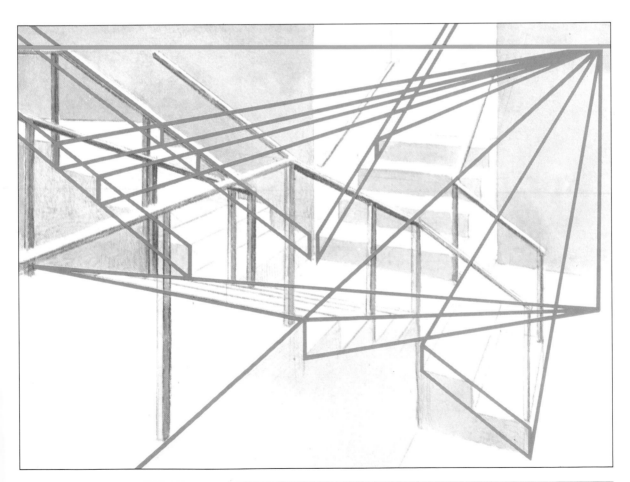

4 Shadows

When you are drawing or painting objectively, shadows cannot be ignored. They make shapes which are compositionally as important and as interesting as the objects from which they are cast (sometimes more so). They can often clarify the shapes and forms of these objects, which may otherwise be ill defined. They can also compel the artist to create tonal pattern, which must be co-ordinated with the other design elements to make an effective contribution to the emotional or descriptive content of the picture.

At various periods in the history of art, shadows have been employed to produce a romantic effect called 'chiaroscuro' (meaning light and shade), which enabled the artist to make some features of his design clear and distinct while others were shaded in gloom. This created a sense of mystery. Rembrandt was one of the great masters of this technique, and although the light and dark passages in his paintings defy perspective logic, they are totally convincing.

Sunlight usually gives better defined shadows over the whole of the picture plane than artificial light and the sun's shadows have a logic which can be seen as incorrect by any viewer if it is ignored. It takes masterful handling (composing) to use such light and shadow creatively and correctly.

'Fleet Sunset' 369 × 419mm (14¾ × 16¾in.). The recession along the beach is here reinforced by the diminishing scale of the mooring posts. Not only do the posts give the feeling of distance, they also help to explain the relative sizes of the boats.

Sunlight shadows

The size and extent of shadows produced by sunlight depend on the position of the sun in relation to the artist and the picture plane, on the time of day, and on the shape of the objects illuminated. An important point to remember about shadows produced by sunlight is that they are continually moving. After a few hours' work in front of a subject in sunlight, you will find that the position and size of the shadows have altered considerably. A few quick notes in a sketchbook from time to time will enable you to decide later where they are most appropriate compositionally.

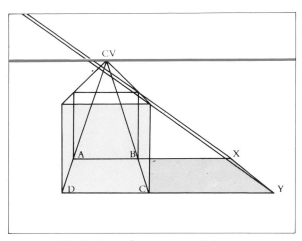

Diagram 56. Shadows of a cube in parallel perspective.

Rays parallel to the picture plane

Shadows cast by the sun's rays falling on an object in parallel perspective on to a level surface are also parallel. The sun's rays in diagram 56 are parallel to the picture plane and the sun is on the left. The length of the shadows is determined by the point at which the sun's rays intersect the lines AB and DC extended along the ground plane, at X and Y.

This applies to any object in parallel perspective. Diagram 57 shows a cylinder. Again, the sun's rays can be traced on the ground plane from lines parallel to the picture plane. In this case, the length of the shadows is determined by the distance from the cylinder's edge, hence the elliptical shape to the end of the shadow. This diagram also shows how the shadow reinforces the description of the shape upon which the sun's rays are falling.

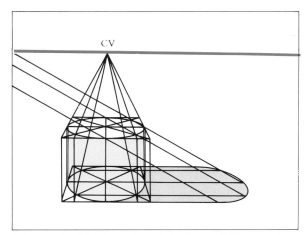

Diagram 57. Shadows of a cylinder in parallel perspective.

This is demonstrated more forcefully in diagram 58 in which a cube has been turned through 45° and projected in oblique perspective. The sun's rays, which are again on the left-hand side and parallel to the picture plane, determine the length and shape of the shadow by their intersection with lines drawn from A, B and C parallel to the ground line. The shape of the shadow explains the form and angle of the cube.

As we have said, obviously the time of day and to some extent the season in which you are working influence the length of the shadows that

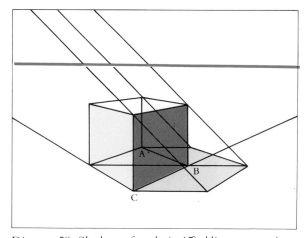

Diagram 58. Shadows of a cube in 45° oblique perspective.

will be cast. In winter, sunlight produces long shadows; a high noonday sun, however, produces very short shadows.

Shadows cast on an inclined slope are longer than those cast on a declined slope. In diagrams 59 and 60, the sun's rays are parallel to the picture plane. To find the length of the shadow on an incline (a pitched roof, for example), first find the horizontal plane. Extend lines from the CV through C and D to the edge of the roof and then around and down the sides of the building until they reach the horizontal line XY (parallel to the eye level). Extend the sides of the chimney AD and BC downwards until they reach the horizontal plane. Extend lines from points W and Z back to the CV; where they intersect AD extended to E, and BC extended to F gives you the forward plane of the shadow. Extend EF to G (drawn back also to the CV) and parallel to the ground plane. G is the point of intersection of the sun's rays, and the bottom extent of the shadow.

Shadows on declined planes are simpler. Extend DC up the slope, parallel to the angle of the roof, until it is intersected by a sun's ray from B at E. Trace from E back to the centre of vision. A line from A to the line ECV gives point F. Then, trace the far side of the chimney up the incline to F. This gives you the length and width of the shadow.

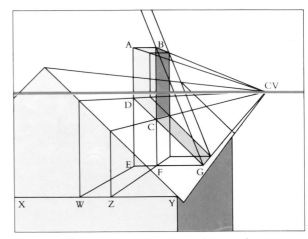

Diagram 59. Shadows on an inclined slope or plane.

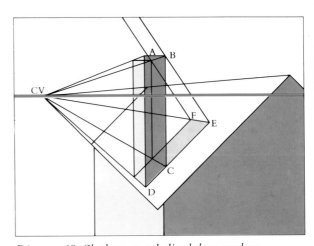

Diagram 60. Shadows on a declined slope or plane.

Sun immediately above the CV

Different phenomena occur when the sun is immediately above the centre of vision. In diagram 61, the sides of the shadow on the ground plane appear to incline inwards and when extended meet at the centre vision on the eye level. If, on the other hand, you were looking down on this cube, you would see the sides of the shadow, in fact, as parallel.

Diagram 62 demonstrates what happens to a wall with doorway and window when the sun is immediately above the CV, seen from directly in front. The sides of the shadow converge along the ground plane to the centre of vision.

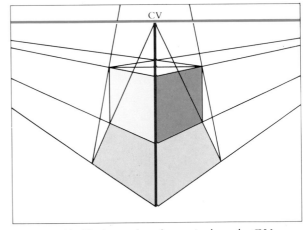

Diagram 61. Shadows when the sun is above the CV.

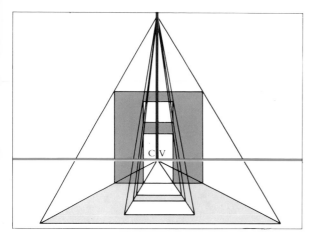

Diagram 62. Shadows of a doorway and window.

Sun to the left or right

Since the sun moves continually, you can't rely on it being directly to your left or right (and parallel to the picture plane) or straight above you. You will often have to cope with it in other situations and may in any case choose, compositionally, to place it elsewhere. In diagram 63, the sun is in front and to the artist's left. What is interesting now is that the vanishing point for the shadow

(VPS) is on the eye level and immediately beneath the sun. It would stay immediately beneath the sun even if the ground sloped. If it sloped upwards, the VP would be above the eye level; if it sloped downwards, the VP would be below the eye level, but in both cases, directly beneath the sun. Because the prism is drawn in oblique perspective, its vanishing points are out to the left and right of the diagram on the eye level.

Diagram 64 demonstrates how you would calculate the length and shape of a shadow if the sun were behind your left shoulder, just opposite to where it was in diagram 63. In this case you have to assume a position of the sun below the eye level; this will allow you to place the vanishing point of the shadow on the eye level. The assumed position of the sun should be as far below the EL as the sun really was above and as far to the right of the CV as the sun was to the left. Rays from the assumed sun to the top of the prism intersect with lines back from the base of the prism to the VPS. This determines the length and shape of the shadow. The vanishing points for the prism are on the eye level outside the diagram area.

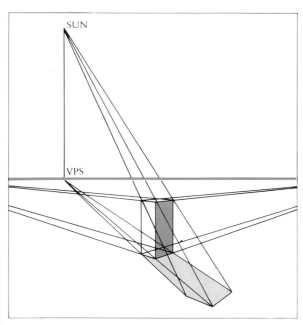

Diagram 63. The VPS is immediately beneath the sun.

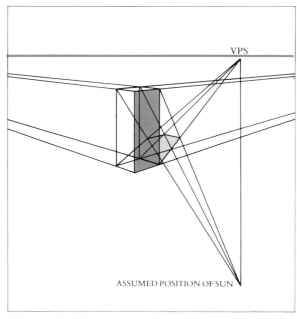

Diagram 64. The sun is behind your left shoulder.

Still with the sun behind your left shoulder, diagram 65 shows what happens to our wall pierced by a window and a door and its shadow. Again, to give the appearance of the sun being behind your left shoulder, the assumed position of the sun is the same distance from the centre of vision to the right as the real sun is to the left.

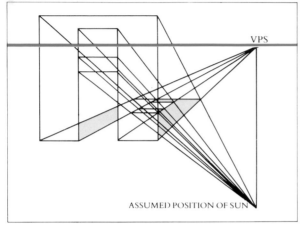

Diagram 65. Again, sun is behind your left shoulder.

Assuming that you are on flat ground, then the sun must be the same distance below the eye level as the real one would appear above. The vanishing point for the shadow is directly above the assumed sun's position on the eye level. The length of the shadows is determined by rays from the sun to the various points of the wall intersecting the vanishing lines to the VPS (shadow).

Shadows of a building with a sloping roof and chimney are illustrated in diagram 66. The chimney's shadow is cast on the sloping roof and on to the level ground. The shadow of the chimney on the roof has a vanishing point as far above the eye level as the vanishing point for the incline but immediately below the sun at VPS1. The vanishing point for the shadows on the ground plane (annotated VPS2) is on the eye level, directly beneath the sun. The length of the chimney's cast shadow was calculated by taking the trace lines of the chimney down to the ground plane and then back to VPS2. Trace lines were then drawn to the right until intersected by the sun's rays at A. It is interesting to note that the shadow of the chimney on the inclined slope of the roof does not appear immediately above the one on the ground plane. You have to calculate each one separately. The drawing is in 45° oblique perspective.

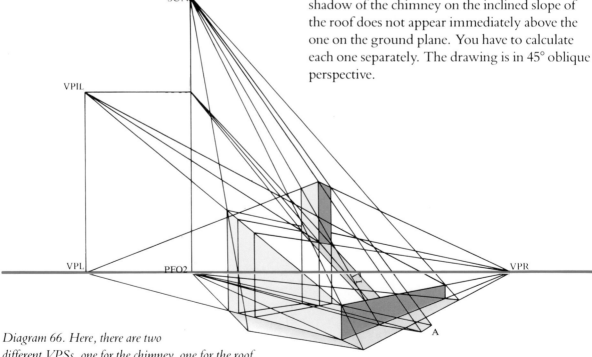

Diagram 66. Here, there are two different VPSs, one for the chimney, one for the roof.

Artificial light

Shadows cast by artificial light radiate from a point immediately below the light itself. These shadows, although well defined when near to, and in the main direction of, the light, become diffused as they get further away. They also are more distorted than shadows cast by sunlight.

Shadows produced by artificial light (the source of the light is indicated in these diagrams as ALS) have vanishing points immediately beneath the light and on the same plane as the objects which cast the shadow. This gives two radiating shadows.

Diagram 67 shows a cylinder. The extent of its shadow is determined by the intersection of the light rays and the vanishing point. The curved top of the cylinder can be determined either from points on the arc, or from diagonals of the square into which it fits (see page 34).

When the objects that cast the shadow are higher than the light source, the vanishing point of the shadow, obviously, is immediately above the light source.

Very often what we see is illuminated from more than one light source, so shadows form improbable shapes and, where they overlap, varied tones. Diagram 68 illustrates how that occurs. The vanishing points for the shadows are immediately below each of the two light sources. The trace and extent of the shadows is determined by the intersection of the light rays and the VPSs. The edges of the shadows appear much softer than those caused by direct light. Also, you will find two distinct tonal values in the area of shadow. The outer, lighter shadow is known as the penumbra and the darker central area of shadow as the umbra. The larger the light source, the smaller the umbra.

You will find a similar effect with a large or long source of light such as a tube light or even (if it is not in direct sunlight) a window with daylight passing through it. Because the light rays are emitted from the whole length of the source, you

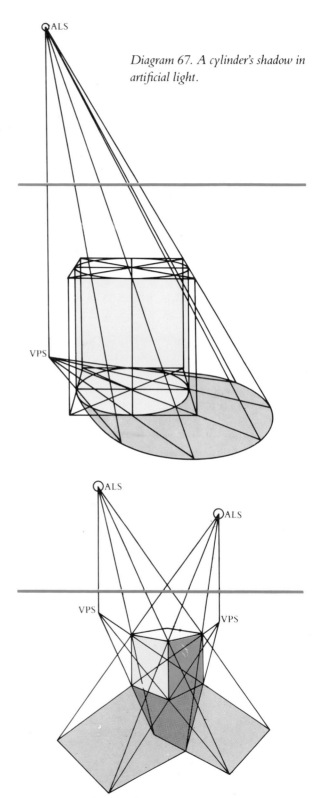

Diagram 67. A cylinder's shadow in artificial light.

Diagram 68. The cube illuminated from two sources.

get what may, at first sight, appear to be a confused shadow. For practical purposes, in a case like this, to construct the shadow take light rays from the centre of the tube or window and

each end. Consequently you will have three vanishing points on the plane on which the object stands, immediately beneath each source point.

A ROOM IN SHADOW

This drawing with furniture reduced to fairly basic shapes shows the shadows produced by artificial light in a common situation. To draw a room like the one illustrated here, a vanishing point for shadows has to be established on each plane. The first is on the ground plane immediately below the light, and a second is on the chimney breast at the same height as the light. This establishes the shadows cast from the picture and fire surround. The third is level with the light

but on the alcove wall, and is used to establish the depths of shadow from the shelving. A fourth, above the door, fixes the length of shadows from the pictures and chest of drawers on the wall facing you. A fifth would be on the far right wall outside the picture plane. This has to be plotted in order to give the length of shadow beneath the curtain. The radiation of shadow, which is the result of one central light source, is very typical of indoor artificial lighting.

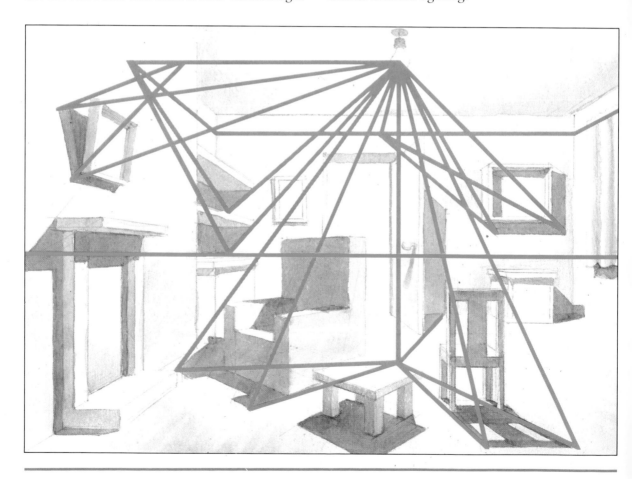

5 Reflections

To many artists the word reflection suggests water. There are, however, many other surfaces that reflect to a greater or lesser degree. The very best reflecting surface is mercury or mirror, but polished metal, a glazed picture or window, some plastics and even gloss-painted surfaces will give interesting reflections. Wet slates will reflect chimneys and wet pavements, figures and lampposts, lights and anything else on them. Sand along the shore, when wet, also gives a reflection. Often these surfaces are not level and slope at angles, which can complicate the reflection, but once the principles are understood the reflected shapes are not difficult to determine.

Agitated water reproduces images at improbable angles, the concavities actually reflecting objects the right way up, while swirls of lines cross, recross or zigzag across the surface. Surfaces are sometimes classified as producing regular and irregular reflections, but it is often difficult to know how to differentiate. Here, we will discuss flat water as a reflecting surface but rippled water is a large and complex subject. One of the major attractions of water that is near is that it reflects less light and, because it is transparent when clear, the bottom becomes visible (if you are in deep water, it takes on the hue of the ocean). The further away you view the reflection the clearer it appears. Vertical objects appear better defined, whereas horizontal ones may not seem to be reflected at all. Lights (such as the moon) on still water give a constant width reflection.

'Low Tide' 232 × 345mm (9¼ × 13¾in.). This chalk drawing on pale blue paper was done quickly on the quayside at Looe in Cornwall. The very shallow water reflects the warehouses and the high harbour wall.

Reflections in water

Most of the examples given here are illustrated in relation to boats, since they are more often associated with water than any other objects.

An object reflected in water is seen as far below the surface as it is in reality above. The reflecting ray to the eye cuts the surface and produces an angle (the angle of reflection, R) which is equal to the angle made from the point on the surface to the object (the angle of incidence, I). This principle governs all reflections, no matter what size the objects are or how far away they are. This is shown in diagram 69.

The reflecting surface is not necessarily the eye level, or even the horizon at sea. Diagram 70 shows a navigation mark, which extends exactly the same distance below the reflecting surface as it is above. More solid objects (a mooring post, for example) can create reflections whose sides appear to be of a different length. In diagram 71, for example, A and B are clearly the same length, but C and D appear different. They are not. They appear so because the angles of recession, extended, converge on the eye level at the centre of vision. An object which is not parallel to the picture plane, however (like the length of timber in diagram 72) does have a reflection that is a different length from the object. The reflecting surface is projected forward from the CV to a point vertically below the nearest end of the timber (where a pebble dropped from C would strike the water at E); D is exactly the same distance below the surface. Both the object's and its reflection's lines of direction when extended will, if produced far enough, converge at a point immediately above and below the centre of vision and equidistant from it.

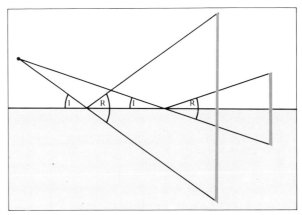

Diagram 69. Angles of incidence and reflection.

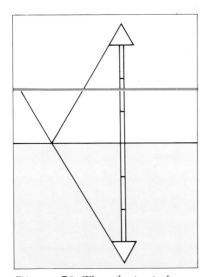

Diagram 70. The reflection is the same depth as the mark.

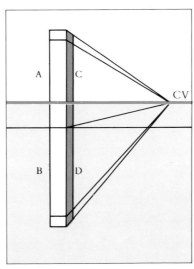

Diagram 71. The reflection appears longer, although it is not.

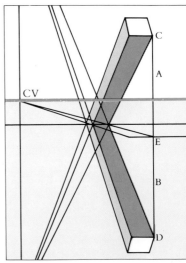

Diagram 72. The reflection is a different length from the object.

Diagram 73 illustrates a very common phenomenon of a flagstaff on the stern of a motorboat. The top of the staff is precisely the same distance above the reflecting surface as its reflection is below. This has to include the height of the stern of the boat. Note how the lines of recession converge on the centre of vision. The reflection of the stern shows a much steeper angle than the object itself because it is in parallel perspective. The same principles apply to buildings on a riverbank or at the seashore. Diagram 74 illustrates equal sized buildings at different distances from a riverbank and their reflections. A piece of the bank has been cut into like a dock to show how this works. Each vertical has to be brought down to the reflecting surface and then continued just as far below as it is above – this includes the height of the bank. Had we not

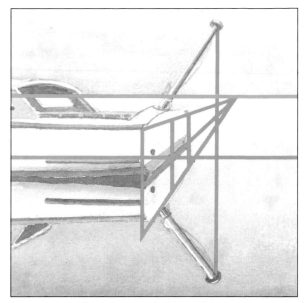

Diagram 73. The reflection of a flagstaff in water.

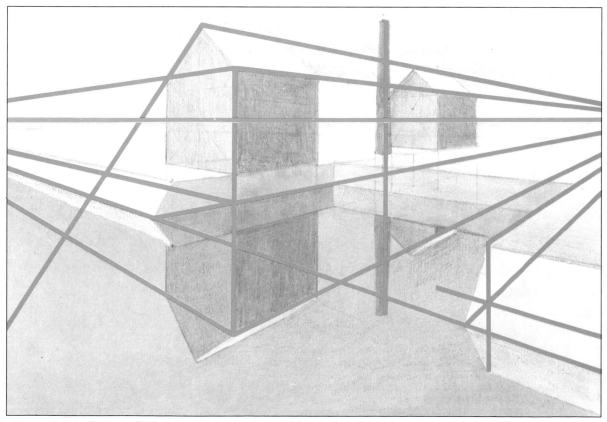

Diagram 74. Reflections of buildings on a riverbank extend as far below the surface as the buildings are above.

cut away the little dock all that would have been reflected of the rear building would have been the tip of its chimney. Note how the reflection of a sloping bank is ascertained by again taking back the level of the reflecting surface until it is vertically beneath the top of the slope. This is then extended the same distance downwards and the points connected.

The reflections of bridges show more of the underside of the constructions than does the direct view. Diagram 75 is projected in parallel perspective, so all the lines vanish to the same point. Those below the reflecting surface are the same distance from it as those above. A bridge in oblique perspective (diagram 76) has vanishing points outside the picture plane. For this reason,

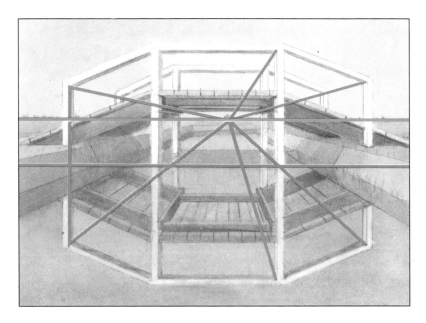

'*Derelict Houseboat' 310 × 455mm (12½ × 18¼in.). This study for a painting gave many compositional opportunities to create improbable shapes from the derelict boat and its reflection in the river.*

Diagram 75. In parallel perspective, all the lines vanish to the same point.

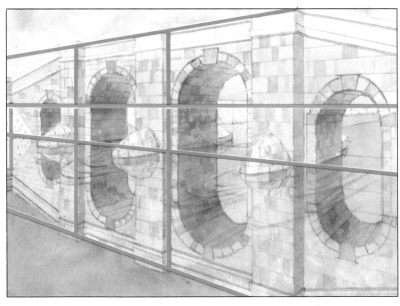

Diagram 76. In both parallel (above left) and oblique perspective (left), more of the underside of the bridges than the direct view is visible.

we can see through the arches. Each arch was constructed from a half square in perspective (see page 34). From then on, the construction is the same as for the bridge in parallel perspective.

Reflections on a wet surface – the reflection of a chimney on a sloping wet roof, for example – give shapes rather like shadows. The area of the reflection is determined in the same way as described in diagram 59. The only difference is that the reflecting surface slopes at an angle and the object is vertical. The easiest way to cope with this is to turn your drawing on its side and visualize the reflecting surface as being level, with the chimney tilting.

When the eye level is below the roof, it is still easier to turn your drawing on its side.

Reflections in glass

Reflections in a mirror are rather like looking through a hole in the wall into another room. The halfway marks between objects and their reflections occur on the mirror wall. Once you have established these marks, use a pair of compasses to describe an arc from the object to its reflection. In parallel perspective, everything slides across from the room into the looking glass. Don't forget, though, that objects will be laterally inverted: the position of the door knob changes, and you see the front of the chairback in the room and its back in the reflection. Remember too that in this situation the angles at which pictures tilt will be reversed.

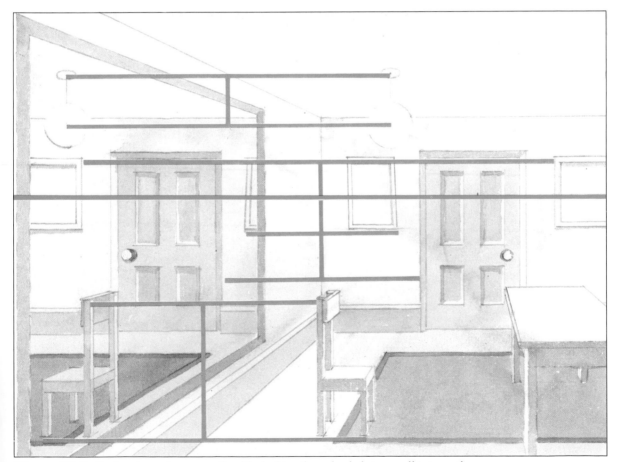

Diagram 77. Reflections in a mirror are rather like looking through a hole in a wall into another room.

6 Composition in practice

It is impossible to place a line on a piece of paper without attempting to draw it in the right place. All pictures have a compositional element. They have in common a sense of the third dimension and are strengthened by the feeling that the design and drawing go on behind the picture plane.

One of the most emotive elements of composition can be the planes which direct our eyes back into, up and across the picture. For this reason, planes are well worth establishing very early in your design, in fact second only to the horizontal and vertical arrangement of shapes and other main movements within the design and the shape you consider best communicates what you have to say.

Your picture's unity (which includes the shapes, tones and colours you use) is indissolubly linked to what you have to say. Remember that it is better to say one thing strongly and unequivocally than to try to say many things. That approach can make the painting fussy, splintered and without unity. Even a painting of a single object needs composing so that the very character and essence of the object are distilled in every shape. Consider your viewpoint, try sitting low on the floor or ground, look at your subject through undergrowth or the back of a chair. Climb high, sit on a table and look down upon your subject. See it in full light with the sun or a window behind you, or stand your subject directly in front of the light. Each position will have something of interest, so choose what, to you, is most exciting and best communicates your intentions. Make sketches, then detailed studies from nature and finally reconstruct the experience into a composition, when all your knowledge and skills of perspective and composition can be brought into play.

The advice and illustrations that follow will help you to employ your knowledge of perspective to create satisfying and meaningful pictures. However, the finest study of composition is to look closely at your favourite paintings by great masters. Trace the designs, find the Golden Sections, then the proportion of the rectangle, then the linear structure. Determine the eye level and principal vanishing points by tracing back the lines of recession, then look at the tonal shapes and masses. These studies will demonstrate that there are as many ways of composing as there are artists: the suggestions given here should not be seen as rules but as guidelines.

Ken Howard 'Saskia, Morning Light' 600 × 500mm (24 × 20in.). This masterly painting is held together by a well-considered geometric design. Although light is as much the subject of the painting as the model, there is a well-conceived spatial relationship between the two- and three-dimensional aspects of the picture. It is interesting to note that the vertical division of the composition is broken by the bent legs of the model, giving excitement to the painting. Note too how the areas of greatest highlights are juxtaposed against the darkest tones and perfectly balanced. There is also a subsidiary linear rhythm of light lines. The light shining on the model's chemise is echoed on the bottle on the table in the foreground and adds a further highlight to the painting.

Creating space

You have probably used, and must certainly have seen works by artists who use, the device illustrated in diagram 78 – putting one object in front of another – to create a feeling of space. By overlapping these shapes a sense of recession is created. This can, however, be ambiguous: you may just be putting a series of inverted 'L' shapes together. To give the impression of putting flat squares one in front of the other, another element is needed. Employing simple parallel perspective in the design, however, leaves no doubt which form is in front of the other and what that form is. Although cubic shapes are used in diagram 79, the principle can easily be applied to a sky filled with great cumulus clouds one in front of another, for example.

Symmetry and balance

Total symmetry and balance, although a common compositional ploy, need not be shunned. Many great pieces of architecture are designed symmetrically and it was used extensively in the fifteenth and sixteenth centuries for paintings of crucifixions, annunciations and other religious subjects. In diagram 80, the fulcrum (F) locates what we know instinctively as the centre of interest. This is a very convenient point around which to compose and on which to centre the action of a painting. It may be at the centre of vision or fulcrum of a mechanically structured design, or at the intersection of the important dividing lines of the painting (see pages 13–15). Many ploys can be used to assemble the directions and forms to direct attention to this spot. There

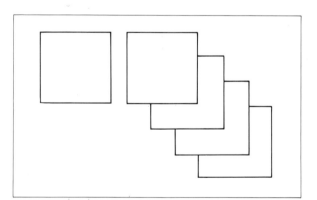

Diagram 78. Overlapping helps to create recession.

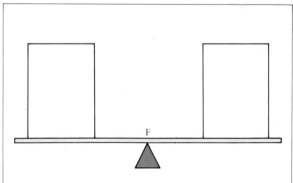

Diagram 80. A completely symmetrical arrangement.

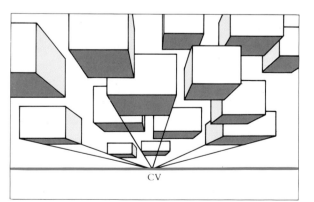

Diagram 79. Parallel perspective reinforces it.

Diagram 81. How to use the arrangement above.

may be possibly very little of importance at that point, it could just be a pinion, or it may be the most interesting point of the picture.

In diagram 81, the fulcrum, the centre of vision and centre of interest are focused at this one point.

Diagram 82 shows an alternative way of achieving equilibrium. The greater mass has the shorter arm of leverage, and the smaller form has the longer arm. This ensures that they remain in balance. In a composition based on this framework (diagram 83), the centre of interest is at the fulcrum and the most compelling centre of interest of all is employed, one of figures.

However small a figure is in a composition, it commands greater attention than more inanimate and elaborate forms. If you link a figure with the fulcrum and/or centre of vision, the eye gravitates straight to it.

In diagram 84, the centre of interest is again at the centre of vision and fulcrum. The mass nearest the fulcrum is hanging below the horizon and is a satisfactory balance to the object above it.

These masses can be made to balance by not necessarily being of greater or smaller area but by being of light or dark tone, or of subdued or vivid colour, or of intense subject interest and detail.

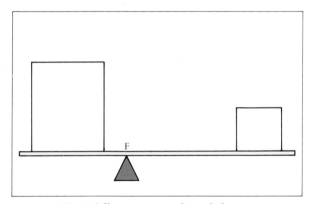

Diagram 82. A different way to achieve balance.

Diagram 83. How to use the arrangement on the left.

Diagram 84. Here, the centre of interest is at the centre of vision and fulcrum, but the larger mass (the boat) is below the horizon and balances the smaller mass above the horizon.

Achieving movement

There are many interesting possibilities in giving a painting or drawing movement. In a static piece of work actual movement is out of the question, but skilful use of shapes, repeated with progressively slight variations, will bounce the eye around a composition. Spots of similar colour or tone placed at intervals over the surface of a painting will cause the eye to move from one to the other, and lines, whether real or simply divisions between one tone and another, can compel the eye to move around wherever you wish.

Tone

Distance affects the tonal values of objects, as well as their colours. Before the nineteenth century, painters made distant passages of their work progressively more blue, without understanding the atmospheric changes that made this appear correct. If there were no atmospheric interference with light rays, black rocks, for example, would look black, and snow peaks white. Now we know that the very light and most reflective areas at a distance – snow-capped mountains, for instance – are not modified by the weaker, short-waved ultra-violet colours, so leave the red and infra-red long waves to penetrate the atmosphere. Thus, snow peaks look pink. The very darkest areas which reflect little or no light will appear at a distance lighter than they really are, so that black rocks will look blue. This is because the diffused ultra-violet short waves reach the dark areas, making them look blue or blue-violet. Half-toned colours depend upon the circumstances of light at the moment. If comparatively dark they will appear lighter, if fairly light they may seem warmer and darker.

'Work Boat' 512 × 705mm (20½ × 28¼in.). This study in gouache was composed on location. I chose the viewpoint that I felt showed the character of the boat to best advantage.

Index

Acknowledgements

Swallow Publishing wish to thank the following people and organizations for their help in preparing *Composition and Perspective*. We apologize to anybody we may have omitted to mention.

Unless indicated otherwise, all artwork is by the author.

The Bridgeman Art Library p6 (top); British Library p26; Ken Howard p55; Reproduced by courtesy of the Trustees, the National Gallery, London pp11, 12, 13, 17, 18, 19; The National Portrait Gallery p10 (top); The Tate Gallery, London p15; Valerie Thornton p7.

Thanks to Kenneth Dear for testing the exercises in this title.

The materials and equipment illustrated on page 9 were kindly loaned by CJ Graphic Supplies, 35-39 Old Street, London EC1 and 2-3 Great Pulteney Street, London W1.